JOY, JOY, JOY
Overflow

Lorraine Steele-Deer

Published by:

Editor: Cleveland O. McLeish (Author C. Orville McLeish)

ISBN: 978-1-965635-29-2 (Paperback)

DEDICATION

To the me who needed to hear these repeating and dynamic words, "Joy, Joy, Joy Overflow."

To myself for enduring hard trials, great challenges, tearful battles, deep pain and hurt, yet pushing through and finishing what I started. For the person I was when I started writing this book and the person I am now.

To you, dear reader, for making this journey worthwhile. To all those who picked up this book, may you find the courage, joy, and love contained within these pages.

ACKNOWLEDGEMENTS

Wow! Hallelujah! Thank you, Jesus! You are super awesome in all Your ways, and You have mighty plans. You fill me with joy in Your presence when I spend time in Your Word.

The joy of the Lord has surely been my strength through this whole journey of completing this book. Through the tears, emotional rollercoaster, persecution, discouragement, brokenness, and pain, God, You kept pouring in me Joy, Joy, Joy until it overflows. To God be all the glory!

I am so grateful to my family for their unwavering faith in God, even through the darkest of nights. Surely, we are a living testimony that weeping may endure for a night, but joy always comes in the morning. It is my absolute delight to mention that my son, Emmanuel (13 years old), initiated the concept of my book cover, and my youngest daughter, Gabrielle (11 years old), cleverly created the design. I am still in awe and am so appreciative of their efforts.

Special thanks to Pastor Sandra Dawkins and Apostle Patrick Dawkins of All Nations for Christ Church in Derby for pastoral support. Many thanks to all the other members of my church family who offered prayer and encouragement. I am also grateful to Maureen Mawundura for her prayers, words of wisdom, and practical help.

I would like to thank my publisher, Cleveland Orville McLeish, from HCP Book Publishing for his professionalism and guidance.

I would also like to thank the following ministries for their love and support: Women on the Front Line, Issues and Tissues and Fragrance of Beauty.

Many thanks to everyone who supported me directly or indirectly. May God bless you all.

TABLE OF CONTENTS

INTRODUCTION

I was inspired to write this book by the Holy Spirit in my moments of brokenness and intense emotional oppression. Early in the mornings, at 3 am during a difficult season, I experienced what I called "my hour of visitation," where I would be woken up to spend time alone in the presence of God. Sometimes, as the tears kept flowing down my cheeks, I found comfort in the whispers of God's love and in the power of these words, *"They that sow in tears shall reap in joy. (Psalm 126:5 - AMP). "Weeping may endure for a night, but joy comes in the morning."* These verses remind us to look ahead of our struggles because the tears we shed in our darkest moments of suffering will produce a great harvest of joy. Joy, Joy, Joy to the Overflow!

It is possible to experience joy in difficult times and to have Joy, Joy, Joy to the Overflow, even during pain or suffering. The true definition of joy goes beyond the common explanation presented in a dictionary — *"a feeling of great pleasure and happiness."* True joy is a supernatural flow of strength that revives, refreshes, and restores the soul.

Overflowing joy is more than a happy feeling and a beautiful smile. It is a positive affirmation that comes from the decision to trust God's promises. It requires absolute reliance in a sovereign source of power.

According to Strong's Concordance, *chara* means joy, calm, delight, or inner gladness. It is related to *chairo*, which means to rejoice, and *charis*, which means grace. Therefore, joy means to rejoice because of grace. It is knowing that overflowing joy is a perpetual response to God's grace through Jesus, our Lord and King. It is the amazing grace of God that moves us from the kingdom of darkness into the kingdom of light, where we can experience peace, joy, and abundant life.

Overflowing joy is not based on our possessions or circumstances. It doesn't mean we will never experience pain and trials.

Jesus never promised that our life on earth would be easy, but that doesn't mean there is no joy in serving the living God. Following Jesus is a journey associated with both joy and afflictions, but we should express our grief and pour out our hearts to God. Even during our sorrow and suffering, we can still choose to have joy because of our hope in Christ. From our relationship with Christ, our hearts are being transformed to desire more for the kingdom as we expand in faith from glory to glory.

I am convinced that there are people who suffer far more than others for the cause of Christ. The truth of the matter is that everyone is experiencing some kind of difficulty right now, but the joy of the Lord will supply supernatural strength to overcome the challenges in our lives.

As you read and meditate on the expounding of God's Word in this book, I believe you will experience exceeding great Joy: Joy, Joy, Joy Overflow!

CHAPTER ONE

EXCEEDINGLY GREAT JOY

And Mary said,
"My soul magnifies and exalts the Lord,
And my spirit has rejoiced in God my Savior.
"For He has looked [with loving care] on the humble state
of His maidservant; For behold, from now on all
generations will count me blessed and happy and favored
by God! "For He who is mighty has done great things for
me; And holy is His name [to be worshiped in His purity,
majesty, and glory]. (47-49 AMP)

Overflowing joy! Joy seems to be a small word, but it has the power to release a big flow of energy that can strengthen and sustain us in our daily lives. Expressing joy is fun and helps to improve our health and wellbeing Interestingly, research shows that people who experience more joy are stronger emotionally and are less likely to be negatively affected by stress. They are more likely to bounce back quickly from a crisis because of the constant flow of joy.

Joy has become one of the most important coping skills for me now. When I am faced with stressful situations, I intentionally try to be more joyful. It is important that we allow the Holy Spirit to flow exceedingly great joy to us to help us get through our daily lives. Studies show that joyful people have less chance of having a heart attack, maintain healthier blood pressure, and tend to have lower cholesterol levels. There is research to prove that joy boosts our immune systems, fights stress and pain, and improves our chances of living a longer life. I require it as part of my day, and I would rather start expressing my joy early in the morning and then let it overflow throughout the day. I have come up with an amazing acronym for J.O.Y.: Jesus Over You! Yes, Jesus is watching over you, angels are watching over you, and our heavenly Father, God, has ultimate control over every situation in your life.

The overflowing stream of exceeding great joy comes through union with Jesus Christ, our Lord and King. This is easier to grasp when there is an abundance of good things happening in our lives: good health, good job, good home, good relationships. But what about when things don't seem so good? Jesus says joy is still available to us.

Jesus was a joyful person, and to His disciples, He said, *"I have told you these things so that My joy and delight may be in you, and that your joy may be made full and complete and overflowing." (John 15·11 - AMP)*. The scriptures impress upon us the importance of building our joy on the truth of who Jesus is, not on anything we may find in the world.

By putting our faith in Jesus, we have His joy in us. By trusting in Him as our saviour, our joy is complete. Jesus is the true meaning of the fullness of joy.

What does "exceeding" mean? "Exceeding" – go beyond the usual mark, surpass, transcend, exceed, and excel. We have access to joy in abundance, but a different kind of abundance than what the world looks for in material things. Joy, Joy, Joy Overflow is the supernatural abundance of love, grace, mercy, forgiveness, and ultimately eternal life. Exceedingly great joy is like a river flowing from the heart that comes from knowing, experiencing, and trusting Jesus. When Jesus is magnified in your soul, you will experience a mighty flow of the spirit like a river running through it.

The Magnificat is a beautiful expression of how the virgin Mary magnified God with her soul.

And Mary said,

"My soul magnifies and exalts the Lord,
And my spirit has rejoiced in God my Savior.
"For He has looked [with loving care] on the humble state
of His maidservant; For behold, from now on all
generations will count me blessed and happy and favored by
God! "For He who is mighty has done great things for me;
And holy is His name [to be worshiped in His purity,
majesty, and glory]. (47-49 AMP)

Exceeding great joy happens when we magnify God. When God is honoured to an extraordinary degree, we can overflow with joy. Like Mary, when we accept the awesome privilege of carrying Jesus inside of us, the Holy Spirit magnifies our Joy, Joy, Joy to the Overflow.

When the angel announced the birth of Jesus to the shepherds, he said it was good news of great joy for all the people (see Luke 2:10). When the shepherds saw the star, they rejoiced exceedingly with great joy (see Matthew 2:10). Even the unborn, John the Baptist, leaped with joy in his mother's womb at the coming of Jesus (see Luke 1:44).

The wise men set out on their way. As they went, the star they saw went ahead of them and led them to the place where Jesus was. The Messiah is coming to make everything right and restore all that was lost. These wise men were looking for "the Messiah," the ruler who would come and reign over the world and bring in universal peace. This is the blessed assurance our King brings. That is what leads people to rejoice with great joy, even amid all the sadness and sorrows of life—the apparent reason why the wise men rejoiced with exceeding great joy.

Exceedingly great joy is expressed in the nativity of Jesus in Matthew 2:10, which says, *"When they saw the star, they rejoiced exceedingly with great joy (AMP)."* During Christmas, we celebrate the first coming of the Lord because it is the beginning of the good news. The benefits we gain when God is magnified will lead us to bow down and worship.

"And after entering the house, they saw the Child with Mary His mother; and they fell down and worshipped Him. Then, after opening their treasure chests, they presented to Him gifts (fit for a king, gifts) of gold, frankincense, and myrrh." *(Matthew 2:11 –(AMP).*

What a powerful scene! These wise men fell down to worship baby Jesus. They rejoice exceedingly as they worshiped and honoured Jesus our King with their gifts. From the very beginning of His life, this picture is clear that Jesus is indeed the King of kings. Look at the reality that we see at the end of the Bible. In Revelation, nations, tribes, tongues, and a great multitude are gathered around the throne of God, singing praises to Jesus for His salvation as our King and saviour. We joyfully expect His second coming when He will reign forever, and we will experience the fullness of His joy.

TRUE JOY

God wants you to be joyful. He wants you to experience exceeding great joy. Joy is much deeper than happiness. Happiness is just an element of joy, and joy is a fruit of the Spirit. Happiness depends on external circumstances and situations, but true joy is an overflow of an intimate relationship with Jesus Christ.

So many people spend their entire lifetime without an experience of true joy, even though they appear to be happy. True joy is missing because the innermost being is inconsistent with trusting God. Jesus is the source of true joy in the heart of man. True joy is not possible when we are separated from God. When we repent of our sins and receive forgiveness, Jesus is enthroned; joy overflows and continues to spring forth. When last did you truly rejoice with exceeding great joy?

I pray that exceeding great joy will spring forth like a reservoir from the centre of your heart as you surrender your worries, cares, burdens, hurt, pain, sorrow, fears, and grief to Jesus Christ.

When you do things from your soul, you feel a river running through you—Joy, Joy, Joy Overflow.

Having joy in one's life is something that people all over the world are seeking in their own lives. People want to be happy and full of joy.

CHAPTER TWO

THE JOY OF THE LORD

"And be not grieved or depressed, for the joy of the Lord is your strength and stronghold!" (AMP).

The joy of the Lord is a constant encouragement to rejoice. It stems from an inner strengthening of our relationship with God, our heavenly Father. When Jesus died for us, He restored us to a peace with God that cannot be undone. Your joy rests on God's promises and His faithfulness.

The testimony, "the joy of the Lord is your strength," originated in the book of Nehemiah. Nehemiah was a man of God who lived through the Babylonian exile long before the birth of Jesus. He is best known for the mission God gave him to rebuild the wall around Jerusalem for return to the homeland. He was a godly man who prayed often that God would remember him for doing what was right. He followed God's ways. He stood up against opposition and completed the job God gave him to do.

Nehemiah was obedient to God's instructions, and the Israelites returned to Jerusalem after centuries in exile to rebuild the temple, their community, and the city walls. Yet, they were weary from the hard work, opposition, and arguments. Although God was working to renew His people, the mission team was often weary and discouraged, and joy was overshadowed with threats and mockery. In Nehemiah 8:10, the helpers were encouraged: *"And be not grieved or depressed, for the joy of the Lord is your strength and stronghold!" (AMP).* The people had to be told to have joy in the Lord, as it didn't come naturally to them during those difficult times. I realized joy doesn't come spontaneously to me either. I must be intentional about obeying God's instructions to experience the joy of the Lord.

"The joy of the Lord is my strength" is a powerful declaration of resilience that has deep spiritual significance. It reminds us of the incredible source of strength and empowerment that comes from surrendering to the plan and purposes of God. When we fully trust in Him and rely on His promises, our hearts are filled with joy. When we are faced with challenges and opposition, we never give up! Despite difficulties and overwhelming circumstances, we appreciate our joy in the Lord when our strength is renewed and revitalised. Our confidence, hope, and courage are anchored in the presence of God. Overflowing joy becomes the fountain of our strength.

"The Lord is their [unyielding] strength, and He is the fortress of salvation to His anointed." (Psalms 28:8 – AMP).

The psalmist David tells us of the blessing given to the hearts of people who trust God; God becomes their strength. He doesn't merely *give* strength; He is their strength and the refuge of His anointed. The word "anointed" (*mashiach*) reminds us of the Anointed One, Jesus the Messiah. His anointed ones are secure in the Messiah, and we are therefore strong and safe.

The Lord is my strength, supporting and carrying me on through all my services and sufferings. He is my shield, to protect me from all the attacks of the enemy against me. I

21

have chosen Him to be, so I have always found Him so, and I expect He will always be so.

The joy of the Lord is a constant encouragement to trust in God wholeheartedly. It stems from an inner strengthening of our relationship with the Lord. Your joy rests on the finished works of Jesus Christ.

FIXING YOUR EYES ON JESUS

In life, one of our biggest struggles is to keep our eyes on Jesus more than the circumstances we are going through. This is not an easy mission; it is more often easier said than done. One of the most well-known passages in the Bible when it comes to "taking your eyes off Jesus" is when Peter walks on water. In Matthew 14, the Bible tells us that the disciples were on a boat; they see Jesus walking to them on the lake, and they are terrified.

"Peter replied to Him, "Lord, if it is [really] You, command me to come to You on the water." He said, "Come!" So Peter got out of the boat, and walked on the water and came toward Jesus. But when he saw [the effects of] the wind, he was frightened, and he began to sink, and he cried out, "Lord, save me!" Immediately Jesus extended His hand and caught him, saying to him, "O you of little faith, why did you doubt?" And when they got into the boat, the wind ceased." (Matthew 14:28-32 – AMP).

Peter momentarily had taken his eyes off Jesus and onto the wind and the waves around him. In his moment of weakness, he began to sink. It is easy for us to be hard on Peter for taking his eyes off Jesus in this moment. Likewise, we tend to do the same.

Wow! In this moment of incredible faith, Peter had his eyes on Jesus and was walking on water. Do you remember a time in your life when you trusted God completely and saw God come through in an amazing way? Sometimes I wonder how we can experience the power and provision of God one day and question Him on another. This is the story of our life and all of humanity.

God demonstrates His love towards us by showing that joy does not depend on our circumstances. That is why I need to keep my focus on Jesus so that when my earthly circumstances seem difficult, I remember the suffering Jesus endured on the cross.

Therefore, since we are surrounded by so great a cloud of witnesses [who by faith have testified to the truth of God's absolute faithfulness], stripping off every unnecessary weight and the sin which so easily and cleverly entangles us, let us run with endurance and active persistence the race that is set before us, [looking away from all that will distract us and] focusing our eyes on Jesus, who is the Author and Perfecter of faith [the first incentive for our belief and the One who brings our faith to maturity], who for the joy [of accomplishing the goal] set before Him endured the cross, disregarding the shame, and sat down at the right hand of the throne of God [revealing His deity, His authority, and the completion of His work]. Just consider and meditate on Him who endured from sinners such bitter hostility against Himself [consider it all in comparison with your trials], so that you will not grow weary and lose heart. (Hebrews 12:1-3 – AMP).

Jesus suffered excruciating pain on the cross, but He endured the agony for our salvation. He chose to walk in obedience to God because of the joy set before Him; the joy of reconciling man and God; the joy of conquering sin and death; the joy of the resurrection; the joy of making a way for us to be free and experience new life. He conquered and overcame the enemy so we will not grow weary and lose heart. We can experience joy during our worst circumstances because He is with us.

You experience overflowing joy when you are assured that no matter what you are faced with, Jesus will carry you through. Overflowing joy comes from fixing our eyes on Jesus instead of worrying about the situation. We can trust Him no matter what is going on in our lives because God already knows the end from the beginning.

We choose to fix our eyes on Jesus.

"..for the joy [of accomplishing the goal] set before Him endured the cross, disregarding the shame, and sat down at the right hand of the throne of God [revealing His deity, His authority, and the completion of His work]." (Hebrews 12:2b – AMP).

The storms of life are going to come, and we will be challenged to keep our eyes on Jesus. The sooner you remember to shift your gaze back to Him, the more your joy will overflow. You can find out what it means to shout, *"The joy of the Lord is my strength."*

CHAPTER THREE

SHOUTS OF JOY

"When the trumpets sounded, the army shouted, and at the sound of the trumpet, when the men gave a loud shout, the wall collapsed; so everyone charged straight in, and they took the city." (Joshua 6:20 – AMP).

There is great power in a shout that commands attention. A shout releases energy, boldness, and passion, and changes the atmosphere. A shout can be a powerful prophetic and faith-building act that declares things that are not as though they were.

Now, all of us can shout to demonstrate enthusiasm, confidence, and overflowing joy. If we have voices, we have all shouted many times, for numerous reasons and on many occasions. We have shouted in the overflow of great joy. We have shouted in the tension of competition and in the triumph of victory. Sometimes, in moments of disagreement, danger, and anger, we shout to express strong emotions.

We rarely shout alone because shouting is predominantly shared as a communal expression, like laughing and singing. Shouts of praise is encouraged in the Bible with singing, because these are overflowing expressions of joy in God.

Perhaps you were brought up being told to "Keep your voices down," keep it under control, but Psalm 100 tells us to shout and make a joyful noise to the Lord in thanksgiving.

"Make a joyful noise to the Lord, all you lands! Serve the Lord with gladness! Come before His presence with singing! Know (perceive, recognize, and understand with approval) that the Lord is God! It is He Who has made us, not we ourselves [and we are His]! We are His people and the sheep of His pasture. Enter His gates with

thanksgiving and a thank offering and into His courts with
praise! Be thankful and say so to Him, bless and
affectionately praise His name! For the Lord is good; His
mercy and loving-kindness are everlasting, His faithfulness
and truth endure to all generations." (Psalm 100:1-5 –
AMP).

Even if you think singing is not your thing, you can make a
loud noise. The psalmist calls us to worship God with
gladness—joy—rejoicing. While there is a place for quiet,
reflective worship, rejoicing should be the theme of our
personal and corporate worship. Shout for joy! This is a call
to cheerfulness and excitement—to the kind of energetic
praise that wells up within you to the point that it can no
longer be contained.

Joy, Joy, Joy Overflow is a call for you to raise the roof—to
give God all the worship from your heart. Praise the Lord
for the wondrous things He has done for you—for the
victories that He gives you day by day.

TUMBLING DOWN THE WALLS

A shout leads to our victory over the enemy. The battle of
Jericho was a significant battle the Israelites fought during
Canaan's conquest.

Jericho was the gateway city to Canaan that the Israelites
came to when they entered the promised land. The city of
Jericho was surrounded by walls, so no one was able to get
in, and the walls served as solid protection against attacks.

The gates were locked to keep the Israelites out (see Joshua 6:1). This moment is incredibly important because the Israelites finally entered the land promised to them by God, and they went on to conquer the first city along their journey. The fallen walls of Jericho became a key affirmation that God was fulfilling His promises and that God would be with them as they took possession of the promised land.

Joshua gathered the army and priests just as God instructed. For the first six days, the armed men marched around the city once while the priests had trumpets and carried the ark of the covenant. They did this for six days. On the seventh day, as God instructed, they marched around the city seven times. The priests blew their trumpets, and the army gave a loud shout.

"When the trumpets sounded, the army shouted, and at the sound of the trumpet, when the men gave a loud shout, the wall collapsed; so everyone charged straight in, and they took the city." (Joshua 6:20 – AMP).

This powerful verse serves as a reminder to us today. Amid trials and challenges, we can find strength not in our own efforts but in the joy that comes from obeying the Word of God. Shouts of joy may have seemed like an irrational approach to tumbling down walls, but Joshua led the Israelites to do what God had instructed. For the Israelites, this was an amazing victory by the power of God through faith and obedience. It is the joy of the Lord that empowers us to face difficulties, overcome insurmountable obstacles, and still persevere in faith.

The Israelites could have marched around the walls of Jericho a million times. They could have blown a thousand horns and shouted until they lost their voices, but without God's power, the walls of Jericho would never have fallen.

We are not entirely self-sufficient; we truly need God. We need God to win our battles, to empower us to love others, to overcome obstacles, and to make a lasting impact in the world. We need God in our friendships, careers, marriages, and families.

Walls are spoken of throughout much of the Old Testament. Generally, walls are used for protection, to separate groups of people, and to create a place of safety from each other. Some walls were so thick that entire communities were built on top of them. People lived on top of the walls so they could see anything coming. Some walls were intentionally built to divide and separate people from other groups or tribes.

In the same way physical walls are constructed, we often build spiritual and emotional walls to protect and close us off from other people. But too often, walls built for safety become so confining that they do not allow the inner man to be challenged, stretched, or confronted.

Are there any walls preventing you from entering the riches of God's promises? Protective walls often become strongholds in our lives, but shouts of joy can pull down strongholds. The name of Jesus pulls down walls. As we lift His name in worship and praise and let our hearts sing to our maker, we will see confining walls in our lives come tumbling down. Some walls may be fragile and easily dismantled, while others may need to be attacked with shouts of praise. Some of our walls may be so thick that they need blasts of shouts to see them smashed.

The fall of the walls of Jericho is a grand reminder that God fulfils what He promises. A lot of time passed between when God initially promised the land to the Israelites and when they entered and claimed that land. It doesn't matter how long it takes; God will always fulfil His promises. God is faithful, so we can keep rejoicing while we wait for the walls to tumble down.

Some defensive walls are erected so our pain can be hidden or so that we can play it safe. Most walls keep us from expressing joy to the Lord. But these walls are breaking and tumbling down through shouts of praise and joy in the Holy Ghost. Shout for joy because the walls are coming down!

CHAPTER FOUR

JOY COMES IN THE MORNING

Sing to the LORD, O you His godly ones,
And give thanks at the mention of His holy name.
For His anger is but for a moment,
[a]His favor is for a lifetime.
Weeping may endure for a night,
But a shout of joy comes in the morning.
Psalms 30:4-5 AMP

For some people, a morning routine may be perfectly planned and precisely organised, but for many, mornings can be rushed, chaotic, and a little something like this: hit snooze multiple times, roll out of bed, jump in the shower, and maybe grab a bit of breakfast before running out the door or logging on for work. However, spending time in the morning with God often sets the tone for the rest of the day.

I just love early mornings! This is how I maintain my personal relationship with God. I often tell myself that I need to spend time in the Word, praying and listening to the Holy Spirit, who is my helper, teacher, guide, and counsellor. I must charge my spiritual battery enough to start the day. Often, I ask the Lord to grant me the desire to get drunk in the Holy Spirit before 9 am. I want to adapt the experience in the book of Acts where they were considered "drunk in the spirit" after encountering God's presence. The apostles were overflowing with joy and had a deep passion to preach the gospel in a very powerful way.

One of the most prominent uses of morning in the Bible is as a time for prayer and communion with God. Mark 1:35 tells us: *"Very early in the morning, while it was still dark, Jesus got up, left the house and went off to a solitary place, where He prayed." (AMP)*.

This verse describes Jesus Christ waking up early to spend time in prayer, emphasizing the importance of beginning the day with spiritual reflection and solitude. Jesus chose to rise while it was still dark. He embraced the early morning. May we learn from Jesus the opportunity of early mornings to spend time with God. Jesus declares himself as the "bright morning star" (*see Revelation 22:16*) who shines on us every day. As night falls away and a new day dawns, the morning star is the most beautiful. The darkness of this world must give way to the brightness of God's glorious kingdom. I pray that Jesus himself will capture your attention in the mornings and give you a new experience of Joy, Joy, Joy Overflow.

Morning routine is incredibly important for our health and wellbeing, especially for people who often face hectic schedules. Starting the day with prayer or meditation can set a positive tone, enabling us to focus on faith and purpose before the cares of the world confront us. Establishing a morning routine that includes prayer, reflection, and gratitude can be spiritually enriching. Let me encourage you to set aside time each morning to connect with God, and you will receive clarity, peace, and direction daily.

The manifestation cf morning often signifies new beginnings, hope, and renewal. The Bible is loaded with references to the morning, both in a literal sense and as a powerful metaphor for spiritual awakening and divine presence.

I will extol and praise You, O Lord, for You have lifted me up, and have not let my enemies rejoice over me. O Lord my God, I cried to You for help, and You have healed me. O

Lord, You have brought my life up from Sheol (the nether world, the place of the dead); You have kept me alive, so that I would not go down to the pit (grave). Sing to the Lord, O you His godly ones, and give thanks at the mention of His holy name. For His anger is but for a moment, His favor is for a lifetime. Weeping may endure for a night, But a shout of joy comes in the morning. (Psalms 30:1-5 – (AMP).

The imagery of night and morning symbolizes the move from darkness (trouble or grief) to light (joy and renewal), reinforcing the belief in hope and redemption. This message is particularly meaningful for those experiencing hard times, serving as a reminder that pain and suffering are not permanent and that overflowing joy will follow. The truth is that God's compassion and relief are never far, even in the darkest times. There is a correlation between the magnitude of difficulties and the enduring grace of God. It suggests that hardships are temporary and that God provides comfort and joy after periods of sorrow.

Here is a deep expression of enduring hope. As painful as a season may be, it is only a season. Life has twists, turns, ups, and downs, and although we may suffer through dark nights, morning will come. We are to sing to God and worship and praise Him. When we are silent and our hearts turn away from worship, we are escaping the experience of overflowing joy.

It is good to acknowledge daily provision from Father God and not to worry about tomorrow. In a world full of anxieties and uncertainties, this perspective is needed. Trusting in daily mercies and provision allows believers to live more fully in the moment, with a sense of trust and security in God's plans.

This world gives us many reasons to despair; heartaches, disappointments, grief, and betrayals can leave us feeling crushed. Dark nights can last a long time, but they are never permanent for those who are in Christ Jesus, for joy always comes in the morning.

Several passages depict mornings as transformative periods symbolized by divine revelation and significant events. For instance, Mark 16:2 says, *"very early in the morning the first day of the week, they came unto the sepulchre at the rising of the sun." (AMP)*. This verse captures the moment when Mary Magdalene and the other Mary discovered Jesus' resurrection, the most powerful moment in history, highlighting morning as a time of miraculous revelation and newfound hope.

Morning is a significant time for prayer, reflection, transformation, and renewal. Whether by starting the day in prayer, trusting in daily providence, or seeking spiritual discernment, embracing the biblical principles associated with morning can lead to a more spiritually enriched life. As we navigate our daily routines, remember that each morning brings a fresh opportunity to exercise our faith in God and align ourselves with His will.

THE RHYTHM OF FAITH

In all aspects of our lives, faith is like a tide that flows high and low. It rises and falls in a rhythm and manifests in different currents and measures depending on our circumstances.

Faith has varied rhythms, moving between assurance and uncertainty, fluctuating in its patterns. The rhythm of faith controls our spiritual environment and synchronises with all of creation. Just as each note in a symphony is part of the harmony and rhythm of the composition, the rhythm of faith produces the harmony of joy that only God establishes. We must yield to the presence and supremacy of God to experience overflowing joy in our daily lives.

Instead of hopelessness, we have His promise that He will make all things work together for good for those who love God and are called according to His purpose (see Romans 8:28). Only God can take the very bad and transform it into something very good. God can take what is meant for evil, turn it for good, and bring beauty from ashes. In this, we see how often there is a connection between great suffering and great creativity, between great loss and great joy.

The reality of joy comes in the morning after a hard night of weeping. Many of the Psalms move back and forth between lament, even complaint against God, to praise and joyful thanksgiving. I have come to believe that that is often the rhythm of faith.

As the psalmist says, *"O LORD my God, you have turned my mourning into dancing; you have taken off my sackcloth and clothed me with joy, so that my soul may praise you and not be silent. O LORD my God, I will give thanks to you forever." (Psalms 30:11-12 – (AMP).*

Surely, you can see the rhythm of faith in Psalm 30. The back and forth between sorrow and joy of this Psalm mirrors real life, whether it is the life of an individual, life as a family, or the life of a nation. We face times of testing, profound challenges, and weeping for what has been lost, but also times of rejoicing for what has been restored. We overflow with joy for what has been given to us by God's grace.

The Bible has far more to say about rejoicing than it does about weeping. Paul admonishes us to *"rejoice with those who rejoice, weep with those who weep." (Romans 12:15 AMP)*. That is what the relationship of joy in a community looks like, and it is a good one because we do not live out our circumstances alone but in community. Anybody's suffering or hardship is ours. Anybody's joy is our joy. We share it, feel it, and in sharing both the weeping and the rejoicing, our bonds of love and compassion deepens and grows.

God is sovereign and has a rhythm of faith that cannot be prevented. All creation is included in the rhythm of God. From the beginning, no power has existed to interrupt God's ever-moving, ever-flowing spiritual harmony of weeping and joy.

HOPE IN THE PLANS OF GOD

You can always find hope in the promises of God and the power of His name, knowing that in your darkest nights, hours of fear, and moments of greatest uncertainty, anxiety, and struggle, God is still in control. He has a plan, and that plan is ultimately good.

"For I know the plans and thoughts that I have for you', says the Lord, "plans for peace and wellbeing and not for disaster, to give you a future and a hope." (Jeremiah 29:11 – AMP).

This is a powerful statement that is much more than any prospect of worldly prosperity. Peace is priceless and is vital for our overall wellbeing. The world is a massive warzone, and countries are hoping for a ceasefire and peace. People are dying and suffering every day, but the truth is, our hope is in Christ Jesus the Prince of Peace. Our heavenly Father offered us a permanent and eternal peace plan by sending His Son to die on the cross for the sins of this world. By faith, anyone who accepts God's gift of eternal life will have hope, peace, and joy.

Overflowing joy comes from the assurance that God will fulfil His plans and purposes for your life.

"being confident of this very thing, that He who has begun a good work in you will complete it until the day of Jesus Christ;" (Philippians 1:6 - NKJV).

When Paul thought of the beginning of God's work among the Philippians from day one, he also thought of the day when that work would be completed. He expressed his *confidence* in God's ability to complete that work.

*"It was indeed a **good work** begun in the Philippians and in all believers. The work of grace has its root in the divine goodness of the Father, it is planted by the self-denying goodness of the Son, and it is daily watered by the goodness of the Holy Spirit; it springs from good and leads to good, and so is altogether good." —**Spurgeon***

Have you experienced the beginning of a good work in you so that you are not what you once were? Once you were dead, but now you are alive; once you were blind, but now you see; once you couldn't hear His voice, now you do; once the things that are earthly, now the things of eternity, the kingdom of God, Jesus Christ Himself, the cross, the resurrection—once these things meant nothing to you, now they mean everything to you. Why? Because God has begun a good work in your life and you will experience Joy, Joy, Joy to the Overflow!

CHAPTER FIVE

OIL OF JOY AND GLADNESS

"You love righteousness and hate wickedness; therefore God, Your God, has set above your companions by anointing you with the oil of joy." (Psalms 45:7 – NIV).

The power of oil is simply overwhelming. Oil is one of the most important commodities in the world as it is currently the primary source of energy and power. The "oil of joy and gladness" gave Jesus the power to be victorious. It will also give every Christian the power to stand joyfully or gladly for the things of God. Jesus, the Son of God, knew He was anointed and full of the Holy Spirit with overflowing joy and gladness.

"You love righteousness and hate wickedness; therefore God, Your God, has set above your companions by anointing you with the oil of joy." (Psalms 45:7 – NIV).

The writer of this Psalm is talking about the king being anointed with the oil of joy by God. The king was anointed with joy because he loved righteousness and hated wickedness. Living in sin and wickedness will only bring about death and destruction. There is no lasting joy in those things. Doing what is right brings life and will last for eternity. You have choices to make in your own life each day.

The way to experience Joy, Joy, Joy to the Overflow is to love God with all your heart, soul, and mind. When you truly love God, you will want to do what is right in His eyes. You will also want to turn away from all wickedness and sin. It is possible for you to be filled with God's joy in your life every day.

A joyful heart overflows with love for the Lord who gave us life. The greater level of calmness in our soul comes from the overflowing love and gratitude to God for His goodness and mercy. We should praise and glorify His holy name as long as we can breathe.

In the presence of the Lord, there is fullness of joy! The greater our peace of mind, the greater our ability to express joy and gladness. Reflecting on the "oil of joy and gladness" gives a deeper understanding of its spiritual significance throughout the Bible. It is more than just an ancient practice; it is a timeless symbol of divine joy, favor, and holiness that continues to resonate with believers today.

One of the reasons I have been able to come through trying times and manage all the responsibilities of family life and community work is that I have learned how to receive a special anointing from the Holy Spirit to do it. I have discovered that when I am experiencing pain and distress, there is an anointing of overflowing joy that the Lord releases that gives me strength and courage. That special anointing that I receive from the Holy Spirit flows out of my innermost being, especially when I feel like giving up. Though I have faced overwhelming obstacles, I am still advancing the kingdom of God because of the supernatural Joy, Joy, Joy that Overflows.

FULLNESS OF JOY

God wants us to be "full of joy"; not half empty or half full, as people often view a glass as a reference to problems in life. The fullness of joy is realistic and is not a mere imagination of a glass with a half measure. I encourage you to look at the front cover of the book again and see what I mean by fullness to the overflow. Jesus came into this world that we might have life in all its fullness (see John 10:10).

Joy flows from being in God's presence and receiving His love and amazing grace. With gladness and rejoicing, we can enter the presence of God, day or night, and find fullness of joy simply because we are children of God and we have a personal relationship with Jesus.

King David said in Psalm 16:11, *"You will show me the path of life; in Your presence is fullness of joy, at Your right hand there are pleasures forevermore." (AMP)*.

Joy is a supernatural flow of the presence of God. It is something that remains inside of us no matter what is going on in our lives. We receive our joy from the holy anointed one: the Lord Jesus Christ. It was deposited within us by the Holy Spirit when we were born again. We are anointed with oil by the power of the Holy Spirit. He sets us apart and empowers us for God's use.

In the Old Testament, when an individual was being anointed, oil was poured upon the head. King David declared, *"You prepare a table before me in the presence of my enemies. You have anointed and refreshed my head with oil; my cup overflows." (Psalm 23:5 – AMP)*.

When someone was anointed, they were understood to be positioned, placed in authority, and ultimately set apart for a specific purpose. The oil was a mark of power, of God's call, especially since the kings were anointed. The anointing oil was a foreshadowing of the Holy Spirit—just as oil was poured from above and onto the head of those appointed, so the Holy Spirit is poured out on those who serve the King of kings, Jesus Christ, who is the anointed one.

"The Spirit of the Lord is upon me, because he hath anointed me to preach the gospel to the poor; he hath sent me to heal the brokenhearted, to preach deliverance to the captives, and recovering of sight to the blind, to set at liberty them that are bruised," (Luke 4:18 - KJV).

When we allow the Holy Spirit to anoint us with the oil of joy and gladness, even during the most difficult times in our lives, we will experience Joy, Joy, Joy to the Overflow.

When the 120 believers were filled with the Holy Spirit in Acts 2, the joy of the Lord was overflowing. That is why the people thought they were drunk. The church became full of joy; they began to impact those in Jerusalem. Then, it continued to spread to other Jews and Gentiles until, eventually, the gospel of Jesus Christ was spread throughout the world.

This anointing by the Holy Spirit with the oil of joy and gladness began to capture the attention of the lost and attract them to Jesus. When you put on the garment of praise and

47

allow the oil of joy to flow in your life, your joy will be full so much that it will overflow to others. So, let the Lord anoint you today with the oil of joy and gladness. I am personally convinced that this same anointing will not only change the church but also touch and impact the world.

CHAPTER SIX

JOY IN THE FRUIT SMOOTHIE

"But the fruit of the Spirit [the result of His presence within us] is love [unselfish concern for others], joy, [inner] peace, patience [not the ability to wait, but how we act while waiting], kindness, goodness, faithfulness, gentleness, self-control. Against such things there is no law. (Galatians 5:22-23 – AMP).

My six-year-old grandson, Emileo, is very curious and spontaneous with questions about God, and he will not stop until he gets answers. So he asked: *"Can you separate God from the Holy Spirit and Jesus?"* This was the illustration I gave him: *"When you mix water with blackcurrant squash, or any other drink, can you separate it after?"* The answer is NO!

The "fruit of the Spirit" is what happens when the Holy Spirit indwells a believer. The "fruit" is the product of the Holy Spirit's blending of spiritual characteristics in one's heart.

"But the fruit of the Spirit [the result of His presence within us] is love [unselfish concern for others], joy, [inner] peace, patience [not the ability to wait, but how we act while waiting], kindness, goodness, faithfulness, gentleness, self-control. Against such things there is no law. (Galatians 5:22 -23 – AMP).

I call this the "spiritual fruit smoothie." When God's Spirit comes to dwell in us as believers, we will manifest the fruit of the Spirit, which is love, joy, peace, patience, kindness, goodness, faithfulness, gentleness, and self-control. These ingredients are blended or mixed by the Spirit and can never be separated. The fruit of the Holy Spirit serves as a visible witness to others that we have been transformed into something beautiful.

If you believe in Jesus and open your life to the Holy Spirit, you have a distinct advantage over the people who don't know Jesus. That advantage is called the fruit of the Spirit. If you allow the Holy Spirit to blend that fruit smoothie, I assure you that you will experience Joy, Joy, Joy to the Overflow!

Spiritual joy is not natural but supernatural. Something is called natural if we can produce it by ourselves without the influence of the Holy Spirit. Spiritual joy is not the human response to pleasant circumstances. What makes something spiritual is the fact that it is generated by the power of God and fuelled by the Spirit of God.

THE GARDENER

When Jesus spoke to people, He used words and stories that He knew people would understand. He made His stories relevant—using everyday images or everyday situations— to explain something. The metaphor of God as a gardener is used several times in the Bible to help us understand His Word. God in spirit form (Gardener) plants the seed of His Word, which grows and develops in us until the fruit of the Spirit is evident. No one can see how we develop as Christians inside our souls until we manifest the fruit of the Spirit. The apostle John begins his gospel by saying, *"In the beginning was the Word, and the Word was with God, and the Word was God. And the Word was made flesh and dwelt among us." (John 1:1,14a - KJV).*

51

The Word can become flesh in you, and—amazingly—it is just as powerful in you as it is in Jesus. When you have Jesus in your heart, joy will overflow.

Of the many pictures of the relationship between God and His people, the vine and branch analogy highlights complete dependence and the need for constant connection to God through His Word.

God is described as the gardener. He waters and tends the plant, caring for it. He removes negative things in believers' lives, so the remaining branches produce even more fruit. He "prunes" branches to correct His people, shaping them to encourage growth. This was an important encouragement as Jesus was about to depart from His disciples. He would remain united to them and they to Him as truly as branches are connected to the main vine.

Only by union with Christ can any branch bear fruit: once that union is broken, the joy no longer flows.

Though the seed of joy remains, it may not be enough to bear fruits without the help of the gardener.

Jesus explained the parable of the sower by saying, *"The seed is the word of God"* (see Luke 8:11).

Plant the seed of the Word deep in your heart. Let it take root and grow through the thoughts of your mind, and then you will reap the harvest of the fruit of the Spirit.

REMAIN IN MY LOVE

Love and joy are inseparable, and they are securely rooted by God, who is the gardener. The connection between love and joy is that love is the root from which joy becomes a fruit. Joy is God's gracious gift to us as a fruit of the Spirit. It is essential in the spiritual growth of a Christian. Like a seed that grows into a tree, let His Word germinate in you and bring forth fruit that pleases Him. You can never separate the identity of a tree from its fruits. In the same way Jesus, who is the living Word, and the Father are divinely connected through the supernatural bond of love. Jesus said: *"I have loved you just as the Father has loved Me; remain in My love [and do not doubt My love for you]. If you keep My commandments and obey My teaching, you will remain in My love, just as I have kept My Father's commandments and remain in His love." (John 15:9–10 – AMP).*

When we obey God's command to love God, ourselves, and others, we experience the fullness of Joy, Joy, Joy till it Overflows. God's love produces joy. Whether we are giving or receiving love, we can bring a profound sense of joy and happiness. Obedience to His commands and remaining in God's love are connected. Obedience should be a loving response to God's Word—a response that is noticeable by the overflowing of joy.

To experience the fulness of joy, we must believe and follow the example of Jesus. In the face of fierce opposition, Jesus found joy in fulfilling the will of His Father: *"Jesus said to them, 'My food is to do the will of him who sent me and to completely finish his work'" (John 4:34 – AMP).* The point is that obedience stems from love, and love is the source of true joy.

When you plant a wheat seed in a field, you expect to get wheat. When you plant a corn kernel, you expect to get corn. When you plant the Word of God, you are more like Jesus because He is the embodiment of the living Word. Our churches are called to be joyful communities in a world desperately in need of an abundance of joy.

CHAPTER SEVEN

REJOICE AND AGAIN I SAY REJOICE

"The Lord your God is in your midst; a Warrior who saves. He will rejoice over you with joy; He will be quiet in His love (making no mention of your past sins) He will rejoice over you with shouts of Joy." (Zephaniah 3:17 – AMP).

All creation is already caught up in the expression of joy and wonder at the Creator. The earth is full of praising and rejoicing. The mountains and the hills burst forth with joy. The water in the brook is bubbling with laughter. The trees of the forest are clapping their hands. Rejoicing is a divine invitation for us to join the created world in this procession of gladness and praise. It is as though the whole creation is saying, *"What are you waiting for? Don't you get it? You people of faith, you children of God, surely you have more than enough reasons to rejoice as well!"*

The psalmist proclaims it best: *"Let the heavens rejoice, let the earth be glad; let the sea resound, and all that is in it. Let the fields be jubilant, and everything in them; let all the trees of the forest **sing for joy**. Let all creation rejoice before the Lord, for he comes to judge and govern the earth! He shall judge the world with righteousness and justice and the peoples with His faithfulness and truth." (Psalm 96:11-13 – AMP)*.

Our Father in heaven, we rejoice again and again at the wonders of Your creation. With each new dawn, there is an opportunity to praise You. We worship You in the Holy Spirit and in the truth of who You are to us. We declare Your greatness because You have saved us. May everyone worldwide hear the good news that God is wonderful and be joy-full. God is great and worthy of praise! God is the Creator and worthy of honour.

You, our great God, made the heavens and the oceans, the mountains and the meadows, the forests, plains, and deserts. You made each person who walks this earth. So, we shout from the bottom of our hearts: *"The Lord, Yahweh, reigns! He is King! He rules the world!"*

Now, imagine how much joy will be on the earth when all its people cry out when our Messiah Yeshua, Jesus Christ the Anointed, returns from His throne to earth as our King above all kings!

In God's kingdom, joy is not connected to earthly pleasures, even though we can occasionally find a measure of happiness. God wants our joy to be rooted in the saving grace and mercy that grants us eternal citizenship, as recorded in the Book of Life. He told the disciples: *"Nevertheless do not rejoice at this, that the spirits submit to you, but rejoice that your names are recorded in heaven."* *(Luke 10:20 – AMP).*

We see this when the seventy disciples return after sharing the good news about the kingdom of God throughout Jerusalem. They are full of joy, saying to Jesus, *"even the demons submit to us in Your name"* (see Luke 10:17). While being filled with the Holy Spirit and casting out demons is good, Jesus makes it clear that He wants us to find our joy in His saving grace—the kindness that He has extended to us as the final sacrifice, paying the wages for our sins. God wants our joy to be attached to His grace for us and on the works that we do in His name. Having your name written in

57

heaven is a testament to God's grace and a promise of eternal life. Surely, this is a far greater cause to rejoice than any earthly achievement or spiritual power.

JOIN THE CELEBRATION

When Jesus returned to heaven, all of heaven rejoiced with Him because man, once lost, was now redeemed. Jesus paid the great cost of redemption for each soul with His own precious blood—the blood of the Lamb. So, when a sinner repents, Jesus sees this as a time for heaven to celebrate. We join with the hosts of heaven to celebrate every time a sinner is saved.

Consider the profound miracle that happens when one person is rescued from the kingdom of utter darkness and is welcomed into the kingdom of light. If you have placed your faith in Jesus Christ, you are no longer in sin and darkness but now in His kingdom. This is a great joy for His people. Jesus entreats us to join the angels and all of heaven in hosting a celebration when the lost is found.

In Luke 15, Jesus told several parables about something being lost and getting found. When the lost item is found, there is always a lot of rejoicing. With each parable, He stated that the angels in heaven are rejoicing over the one person who repents.

"Even so, I tell you, there is joy among and in the presence of the angels of God over one [especially] wicked person who repents changes his mind for the better, heartily

amending his ways, with abhorrence of his past sins." (Luke 15:10 – AMP).

The parable of the lost sheep is very applicable to the great work of man's redemption. The lost sheep represents the sinner as departed from God and exposed to dangers if not brought back to Him. Christ is earnest in bringing sinners home.

As a mother of five children, I can imagine the sadness if one of my children were to be lost or missing from home. All my children are precious, and I rejoice at their birth and continue to rejoice as they grow and thrive. There is a reason to rejoice over each of them as individuals, and then we join the celebration together as a party. Joy is meant to be full and complete, with nothing lost or missing.

In the parable of the lost coin, that which is lost is a small amount compared with the rest. Yet the woman seeks diligently till she finds it. She finds it. She calls her friends and neighbours to join in the celebration. Joy at finding one lost piece of a puzzle that is needed to complete the picture is joy among the angels at the recovery of a single sinner. Every sinner is part of God's picture of redemptive love.

JOY OF THE REDEEMED

We think about God in a lot of ways, but normally, people don't think of God as joyful. But God does everything for His own pleasure and joy. God has a compelling interest in the recovery of sinners for His own purpose. This is the

59

present and eternal joy of the redeemed. Prophet Zephaniah says in chapter 3, *"The Lord your God is in your midst; a Warrior who saves. He will rejoice over you with joy; He will be quiet in His love (making no mention of your past sins). He will rejoice over you with shouts of joy."* *(Zephaniah 3:17 - AMP).* This is what I describe as "super amazingly awesome" to think that God rejoices over me with shouts with joy. It is about the joy of Lord for the redeemed. I love the "warrior who saves!" The hosts of heaven erupts with joy every time a soul is saved, and a sinner is rescued by Jesus our warrior. That's why there is nonstop joy in heaven because every moment of every day, a sinner is redeemed somewhere. Heaven is in a constant state of rejoicing.

Isaiah 35 paints a vibrant picture of a future infused with the hope of everlasting life and redemption.

"And those the Lord has rescued will return. They will enter Zion with singing, and everlasting joy will crown their heads; gladness and joy will overtake them, and sorrow and sighing will flee away." (Isaiah 35:10 – AMP).

The prophet speaks of a time when restoration and spiritual healing will occur, and joy will replace sorrow. This transformative power of God's redemption serves as a beacon of hope for us today, reminding us that God's love can make the 'deserts' in our lives bloom with new life. This is indeed "the good news" that encourages the fearful and weak to be strong and courageous. God assures His people that He will come with vengeance to save them, providing hope and comfort to those in need.

God promises to fill us with His joy when we seek the Lord. As we look at joy from a clinical perspective, we understand that we will be returning for more treatment again and again as we prove the benefits of joy. We will have Joy, Joy, Joy to the Overflow as we rejoice again and again. In other words, we are creating a cycle of Holy Spirit craving that causes an overjoyed attitude in our lives. In devoting ourselves to prayer, worship, and studying the Word of God, we will experience a breakthrough in our spirit, which causes us to rejoice again and again.

This joy is expressed by the countless multitude standing in the presence of God and the Lamb in Revelation 7:9-10. It is symbolised by the palm branches in their hands. In Israel, palm branches have been used historically for joyful celebrations. The palm branches in the hands of the redeemed and the cherubim surrounding the throne are seen together in their eternal reality: standing in the presence of God in joyful celebration. By the blood of the Lamb, death and darkness have been replaced with life and light in union with Jesus Christ. Sin no longer separates us from His presence. Rejection has been replaced with acceptance. Fear in the presence of God has been swapped with joy. With joy, the redeemed cast their crowns and bow in adoration before the throne of God in glorious celebration to Jesus Christ, the Lamb of God who is worthy.

CHAPTER EIGHT

OVERFLOWING JOY

"Consider it nothing but joy, my brothers, and sisters, whenever you fall into various trials. Be assured that the testing of your faith (through experience) produces endurance (leading to spiritual maturity, and inner peace). And let endurance have its perfect result and do a thorough work, so that you may be perfect and completely developed (in your faith), lacking nothing." (James 1:2-4 AMP)

To overflow means to extend beyond the limits, to be in excessive abundance or more than enough. Overflowing joy comes from a heart filled with perpetual gratitude and an inward contentment that flows in the Spirit. What a joy it is to "flow in the Spirit." It is enjoyable, supernatural, and authentic. It gives us a foretaste of heaven's reality before the throne of God. This is why joy is connected to offering worship and thanksgiving to our heavenly Father, joining all the saints and the heavenly hosts. Overflowing joy has the power to change the atmosphere in our immediate surroundings and beyond. Joy, Joy, Joy Overflow emphasizes the desire to seek the kingdom of God and to impact those we interact with daily.

The overflow of joy is expressed with gratitude and thanksgiving. Gratitude is a deep appreciation of kindness shown by one person to another. It enables us to be thankful in any situation as we develop deeper faith, compassion, humility, and perseverance. True joy is an outflow of an intimate relationship with God, irrespective of the circumstances. The command to give thanks in all things is deeply rooted in Scripture. The apostle Paul wrote to the early Thessalonian church to encourage them in their faith. In 1 Thessalonians 5:16-18, he exhorts believers to: *"Rejoice always, and delight in your faith; be unceasing and persistent in prayer; in every situation (no matter what the circumstances) be thankful and continually give thanks to God; for this is the will of God for you in Christ Jesus."* *(AMP)*.

These exhortations are a great reminder to all of us who are in a personal relationship with Christ Jesus. Prayer should be a joyful experience of having a constant faith-filled conversation with God. This doesn't mean we must be on our knees all day but rather that prayer should be a delightful hobby and a way of life. Prayer must be our number one priority because it is the means of connecting with God, seeking His guidance, and expressing our needs and gratitude. Gratitude can transform our perspective, allowing us to see God's hand at work even in difficult situations. By rejoicing, praying, and giving thanks, we express our joy in a powerful way.

It is not just in 1 Thessalonians where we find this theme of giving thanks in all things. Throughout Scripture, we see exhortations to give thanks in all things, both in good times and bad, and we see examples of gratitude in a variety of situations. The Bible is clear: God wants us to be thankful not just for the good things in our lives but even in the trying times. Paul demonstrated this kind of thanksgiving, often expressing gratitude even while facing persecution, imprisonment, and hardships.

COUNT IT ALL JOY

Generally, the act of counting means to consider an amount, the worth, or value of something by adding it all up. Are you facing trials and challenges in your life? You may find it hard to "count it all joy" because of the many trials you have been facing.

"Consider it nothing but joy, my brothers, and sisters, whenever you fall into various trials. Be assured that the testing of your faith (through experience) produces endurance (leading to spiritual maturity, and inner peace). And let endurance have its perfect result and do a thorough work, so that you may be perfect and completely developed (in your faith), lacking nothing." (James 1:2-4 - AMP).

James, through these verses, points us to the value of our joy—a joy not dependent on our circumstances but a joy that resides within us and can keep us calm even during a storm. Irrespective of the source and severity of the trial, we can remain joyful. Every trial is working out something in us and through us whether we feel like it or not. Seasons of trials can become seasons of in-depth encounters with the person of Jesus through His Word. They can also become moments of transformation and renewal of the mind. It is during your trials that God perfects your patience and perseverance. It can just be God calling you deeper into intimacy with Him through prayer and His Word. It can be what God uses to work on your character so you may become more Christ-like and shine your light brightly to the world.

It is so important to view life's trials and challenges as an opportunity for growth rather than a stumbling block to our progress. But it all begins with a change in our mindset and attitude. We often think trials are unnecessary and daunting. Yet, James tells us to embrace joyfulness when trials come at you from all sides. It is possible to be joyful and experience spiritual growth when facing trials in your life.

You have a new life in Christ and through the sanctifying work of the Holy Spirit in your life.

As you read the final section of this book, I pray that your mind be renewed through the Word of God. Choose to embrace the abundance of joy in your heart today.

JOY FROM THE HEART

You may ask it this way: *"Where can I find joy? How do I know if I have joy?"* Joy flows from your heart; the more your heart is full of joy, the more it overflows. The abundance of joy is evident in your worship to God. If you engage in worship but never feel something flowing from the abundance of your heart, you have not worshipped. Jesus told His disciples that He came so that His joy might be in them and that their joy might be full (see John 15:11). So, if you feel like something is missing, perhaps your heart is not engaged in worshipping God. If your whole heart is not offered freely, it will not overflow with joy.

1 Chronicles 29:9 says, *"Then the people rejoiced because these had given willingly, for with a whole and blameless heart they had offered freely to the Lord. King David also rejoiced greatly." (AMP).*

This is a congregation that is overflowing with joyful expressions. As they bring their gifts and offer them to the Lord, they bounce up and down with excitement. Some are even crying tears of joy as they devote themselves to the Lord.

67

The people of God had given their whole heart to the Lord. He was the centre of their affections. Their worship was not merely a sense of duty but the overflow of delight.

We get the English word for worship from a combination of two root words: worth and ship. When we worship, we are acknowledging the worth of our relationship with Jesus Christ, the Son of God. Our hearts are expressing that He is more worthy than anything or anyone else. Jesus reminds us in the gospels that where our treasure is, there is where our heart is.

When Jesus talked to the Samaritan woman at the well, He told her that worship comes from the inside of us—from our hearts. He shared with her *"...worship the Father in spirit and truth; for the Father is seeking such to worship Him." (See John 4:7-30)*

If you desire to experience "Joy, Joy, Joy Overflow" it is important that you understand that your heart is the centre of true worship.

RIVERS OF LIVING WATERS

The 'rivers of living water' Jesus was referring to is the Spirit of God working in and flowing out of the life of a believer. When Jesus made this statement, He was letting us know He would allow the indwelling Holy Spirit to flow rivers of living waters from within us as promised. This one truth alone is enough to transform your life.

The word *rivers* simply means a constant flow like a flood or an overabundance. Think of any time you have seen torrential rain and the water flowing into the river, creating a powerful stream of water that flows over everything in its path. This is how overflowing joy should be in your life.

What Jesus desires and what should be the case in the life of every believer is that there should be an abundant flow of joy in your life.

When something is flowing, it is not static. It continues moving in the same direction with consistency and energy within the flow. God has given you abundant power, a river of living water that dwells within you in the person of the Holy Spirit. "Rivers of living water" represent the Holy Spirit's presence and power poured out on Jesus' followers. The Spirit's presence points to his cleansing and sanctifying work in the hearts of God's children. The Spirit's power points to the spiritual ability to know, follow, and glorify Jesus and to participate in His coming kingdom. The Spirit's presence and power flow out of the believer's heart like water in a parched world.

For your physical health, drink more water. But for eternal health, accept the refreshing spiritual presence and power of the Holy Spirit in your life today and always.

The exciting part of this truth about the rivers of living waters is that Jesus said this is for whoever believes in Him. This means Jesus intends for you to be a person who

69

overflows with the abundance of the Holy Spirit working in you. This is not reserved for merely a few but is intended for any person who believes. If you are a believer in Jesus Christ, which means He is your Savior and Lord, then the rivers of living water should be flowing from within you. This promise is for every believer. That is why when you understand the rivers of living water, it will change your life. God desires and expects that the Holy Spirit will be abundant in your life, not just a mere presence. Holy Spirit, fill our lives with your presence and power so that Your love may flow from our hearts like streams of water in a dry and thirsty land.

Today's society needs more joy. Joy is such a far cry from the way most people live their daily lives. But the good news is that overflowing joy is possible, even in today's trouble-filled society. Overflowing joy comes when you devote your entire life to pleasing God by doing the work He has given you with all your heart. To every one of us, there is a divine assignment for which we are here on earth. Doing it with all our hearts brings such joy that words can never describe. This joy strengthened Jesus to live the way He lived and die on the cross for our sins. There was a joy set before Him (see Hebrews 12:1-3). Live to pursue true joy. Pray and ask that your joy may be full. In all your joy, you must give God all the glory, and the joy of the Lord will be your strength.

JOY TO THE WORLD

Joy is not just a personal pursuit but a gift we can share with the world. Across the globe, 'Joy to the World' is sung every year at Christmas time to celebrate coming together. It is one of the oldest classic Christmas carols sung every festive season and one of the most beloved. The most published Christmas hymn, "Joy to the World" is not just a Christmas hymn. It celebrates both the first and second coming of Christ as Saviour, Lord and King.

The lyrics of the song "Joy to the World" speak of God's salvation and the wonders of His love. The first stanza rejoices that Christ has already come and invites us to make room for Him in our hearts. The chorus joyfully proclaims that all creation will rejoice when Jesus Christ returns. The rest of the hymn expresses joy that the Saviour will reign on the earth. The curse of Adam will be reversed. He will rule with truth and grace, and all the nations will know it.

The Lord is come, wherever people are baptized in His name, saved by His grace, and rejoice as He reigns among them. The Lord will come as far as the curse is found. Joy to the world indeed.

Joy, Joy, Joy Overflow! We rejoice for the Lord has come. He was born of the virgin, lived a perfect life for us, died for our sins, and was raised to life. He ascended to the right hand of the Father's throne in heaven. We bow our hearts and worship before His throne. We are seated with Christ in heavenly places and have divine access to the throne of grace and mercy.

Lorraine Steele-Deer

When Jesus returns, He will establish His kingdom on earth and bring an end to all suffering. We joyfully sing joy to the world for salvation belongs to our God, who sits upon the throne. J.O.Y-Jesus Over You, Joy, Joy, Joy Overflow!

JOY INSPIRATIONAL QUOTES

"Worry never robs tomorrow of its sorrow, it only saps today of its joy."

—Leo Buscaglia

"Find a place inside where there's joy, and the joy will burn out the pain."

—Joseph Campbell

"If you carry joy in your heart, you can heal any moment."
—Carlos Santana

"The walls we build around us to keep sadness out also keeps out the joy."
—Jim Rohn

"Gratitude can transform common days into thanksgivings, turn routine jobs into joy, and change ordinary opportunities into blessings."
—William Arthur Ward

OTHER BOOKS BY THE AUTHOR

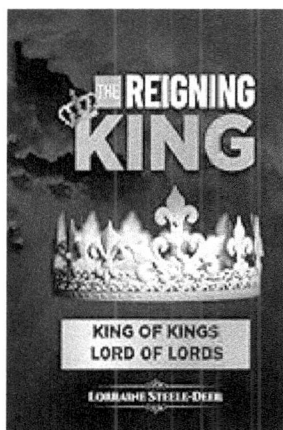

THE REIGNING KING

KING OF KINGS
LORD OF LORDS

LORRAINE STEELE-DEER

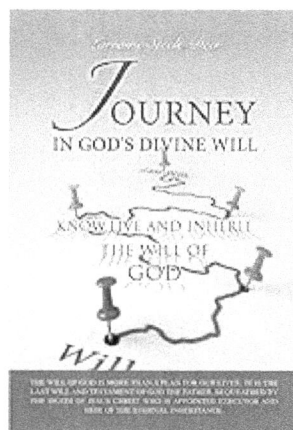

JOURNEY
IN GOD'S DIVINE WILL

KNOW, LIVE AND INHERIT
THE WILL OF
GOD

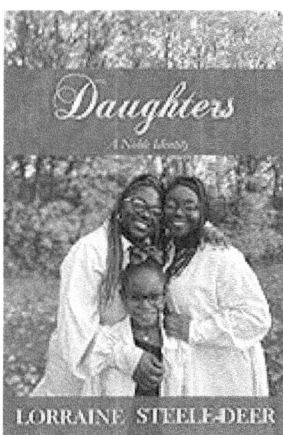

Daughters
A Noble Identity

LORRAINE STEELE-DEER

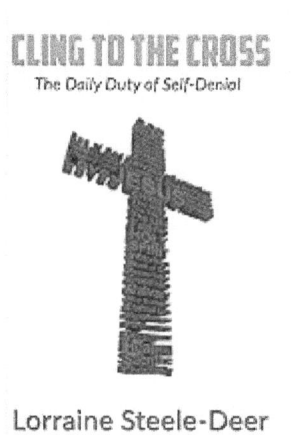

CLING TO THE CROSS
The Daily Duty of Self-Denial

Lorraine Steele-Deer